797,885 Books
are available to read at

www.ForgottenBooks.com

Forgotten Books' App
Available for mobile, tablet & eReader

ISBN 978-1-330-26401-0
PIBN 10005895

This book is a reproduction of an important historical work. Forgotten Books uses state-of-the-art technology to digitally reconstruct the work, preserving the original format whilst repairing imperfections present in the aged copy. In rare cases, an imperfection in the original, such as a blemish or missing page, may be replicated in our edition. We do, however, repair the vast majority of imperfections successfully; any imperfections that remain are intentionally left to preserve the state of such historical works.

Forgotten Books is a registered trademark of FB &c Ltd.
Copyright © 2015 FB &c Ltd.
FB &c Ltd, Dalton House, 60 Windsor Avenue, London, SW19 2RR.
Company number 08720141. Registered in England and Wales.

For support please visit www.forgottenbooks.com

1 MONTH OF FREE READING

at

www.ForgottenBooks.com

By purchasing this book you are eligible for one month membership to ForgottenBooks.com, giving you unlimited access to our entire collection of over 700,000 titles via our web site and mobile apps.

To claim your free month visit:
www.forgottenbooks.com/free5895

* Offer is valid for 45 days from date of purchase. Terms and conditions apply.

English
Français
Deutsche
Italiano
Español
Português

www.forgottenbooks.com

Mythology Photography **Fiction**
Fishing Christianity **Art** Cooking
Essays Buddhism Freemasonry
Medicine **Biology** Music **Ancient Egypt** Evolution Carpentry Physics
Dance Geology **Mathematics** Fitness
Shakespeare **Folklore** Yoga Marketing
Confidence Immortality Biographies
Poetry **Psychology** Witchcraft
Electronics Chemistry History **Law**
Accounting **Philosophy** Anthropology
Alchemy Drama Quantum Mechanics
Atheism Sexual Health **Ancient History**
Entrepreneurship Languages Sport
Paleontology Needlework Islam
Metaphysics Investment Archaeology
Parenting Statistics Criminology
Motivational

The Young Woman as a Bride

THE SUCCESSFUL YOUNG WOMAN

BY

ERVIN F. LYON, Th. M.,

With an Introduction by
KATIE DAFFAN,

Author of "Woman in History," "Texas Hero Stories," etc., and late President of the Daughters of the Confederacy In Texas

RICHARD G. BADGER
THE GORHAM PRESS
BOSTON

1911

COPYRIGHT 1911 BY ERVIN F. LYON

All Rights Reserved

THE GORHAM PRESS, BOSTON, U. S. A.

AN ADVANCE WORD

These words to Young Women are sent forth with the hope and prayer that responses may be found in thousands of hearts throughout the country. The most that could be wished for them is that inspiration and help might come to those whose hearts need only a voice to awaken latent powers for great things in the service of God and of mankind. Should you be helped by reading these messages, let the flame touch yet another life within your circle of influence, to enkindle ambition's conquering fire.

ERVIN F. LYON.

San Angelo, Texas, September 1st, 1911.

INTRODUCTION

THE author of this most attractive and helpful volume makes enduring Love and Faithfulness the glorious qualities of ideal womanhood, and with each subject is a practical and forceful lesson, indicating the author's knowledge of human nature as well as his strength of purpose and deep and abiding admiration for the ideal in woman.

"The Young Woman and Her Education" presents with directness the unquestioned necessity for female education, and the excellent opportunity at the present time, unlike the earlier time, offered to young women who seek recognition in the world of letters.

"The Young Woman and Her Circle of Friendships" clearly and forcibly puts forth our great social obligations and mutual dependence, and the great happiness which comes to a woman from having friends among both men and women.

The author offers great encouragement to those young women who "make their own way in the world" in business or profession, and who are recognized as lifters and helpers, and who are an elemental force and power in our present day progress. As Mother, Wife,

CONTENTS

	Page
The Young Woman and Her Education	13
The Young Woman and Her Circle of Friendships	27
The Young Woman Making Her Own Way in the World	45
The Young Woman and Her Influence	61
The Young Woman and Her Affections	75
The Young Woman Becoming A Bride	85
The Young Woman as A Home-maker	103
The Young Woman in Public Life	119

I

The Young Woman and Her Education

"Having been reminded of the unfeigned faith that is in thee; which dwelt first in thy grandmother Lois, and thy mother Eunice."—II Timothy 1:5.

"And she had a sister called Mary, who also sat at the Lord's feet and heard his words. For Mary hath chosen that good part which shall not be taken away from her."—Luke 10:39, 42.

"A suitable education for each and a Christian education for all."—Hannah Moore.

"Education commences at the mother's knee, and every word spoken within the hearsay of children tends toward the formation of character."—Hosea Ballou.

I

THE YOUNG WOMAN AND HER EDUCATION

THE intellectual advancement of young women is one of the most practical, vital, and far reaching themes engaging the educational world today. Only those who do not think can escape it. The theme lives, throbs, and pulsates with life. One of the surest signs of a nation's development and progress is for it to become genuinely aroused as to the needs of enlightenment among its people. A nation's power rests not with her so called rulers nor with her bands of armed men, but is found in the homes throughout her domain. The homes of her people furnish the nerve and sinew of her strength, while this nerve and sinew are made from the very life blood of the mothers of our country. Hence it is that a little earnest thought upon the necessity of female education will reveal the right view-point, and shed such a lustre of light upon the question that none need err therein.

Let us then turn at once to the practical side of this vital question, and consider first **HER RIGHTS AS TO EDUCATION.** There

THE SUCCESSFUL

was a time when woman did not have untrammeled rights in the intellectual sphere. Her mind and soul were enslaved by the state of a barbaric world, and she was regarded and treated merely as servant,—or worse still, as slave. Every liberty loving heart will rejoice to know that such a day of darkness has gone forever into the oblivion of the past. Under the benign influence of the Christian religion woman is coming into her own. She is now emancipated and given a chance to prove herself the equal of man in mind-strength, and thus lay claim to her privileges for usefulness. In Christianized lands woman is not only being considered the equal of man, but she is regarded his superior in very many things; hence it is that she should have an unquestioned claim in educational pursuits.

Every avenue of learning today is open to her. She is allowed to plead at the bar, permitted to practice medicine, has leave to study the sciences, and full license to work along any and all lines that may be prompted by her desires. History may record the fact that there was a time when the world knew nothing more than class education; that is, there was one kind of education for the children of so called rank, and another kind for the children of peasants. One was educated merely for occupying a

 YOUNG WOMAN

place in society; the other, if educated at all, to occupy the place of slave or servant. Again, we are proud to announce that such a day has passed, and in our fair land especially, opportunities for education are open to all alike. Our young women may turn their eyes towards the halls of learning and satisfy their thirst and ambition for education, and rise higher and higher in the scale of usefulness. Woman is free to choose as she may her life work, and this is more than an ordinary thing. Once in a while now we see the daughter of a capitalist who is thirsting for an education of the highest order; she is longing for knowledge, and so much so that she is fitting herself at the sacrifice of much gay pleasure for a large place in the service of humanity, although she comes from a home of ease and luxury, and ordinarily speaking, ample financial provision is made for her. The world may say she need not bother her brain about much education, yet the desire for a worthy place in the world has laid hold of her and she prefers those things that will fit her for a more important position in the great struggle of life, to the mere glamor of wealth and the glitter of social circles.

We shall consider in the next place, **THE CAPACITY OF WOMAN FOR EDUCATION.** This is today recognized as never before. It is

 THE SUCCESSFUL

seen to be true by provisions now made for her beyond the public school. Parents are becoming anxious to provide for the welfare of the girl as much as for the welfare of the boy. The time was when parents thought the daughter did not need to go to college and be fitted for life work. The boy must always go; the boy must be fitted for some place where he might gain honor and renown. But as to the girl,— as soon as she was through the public school, the next thing for her to do was to get married, and if she failed in this she was to be left a helpless and dependent "old maid," as the world has been cruel enough to call her. It is joyous to note that that day has also largely passed, and to observe that our women are privileged to college life and encouraged to go forward in the things that will so surely fit them for a place in the world's affairs. Again, she is no longer looked upon as helpless if she does not get married. One of the most disastrous things is such an idea in the minds of many of our parents. Some of the most valuable women this world has ever seen chose to remain single. Let the world call them old maids. What mattered that to them? Frances Willard, one of the greatest women this country has ever produced, chose to remain single throughout her eventful life because she was

 YOUNG WOMAN

wedded to her great work. Hannah Moore, the great English educator, remained single all of her days because she had a high and holy mission in the education of the young women of England. We see again, that America's greatest woman philanthropist, Miss Helen Gould, has chosen to remain single that her great heart might serve the whole land.

It is a significant fact that the colleges are raising the standard for women and opening their doors to them as never before. You can now go into the colleges of our country and there find young women literally flocking to them in order to obtain such education as to make them somebody, and that will fit them for a worthy place in life, whether it be in the home, or before the public in some way where they may efficiently work. Then she herself has become aroused as to her ability. Home study, courses of reading, literary clubs, and many choice books are now being read by the women of our land. Searching into the history of the past and into the knowledge of the present, they are becoming prophets of the future, thereby filling a very large place in the affairs of humanity. A striking example of self culture is noted in the case of a woman who had been left an orphan very early in life and had no advantages of education. Later on, when mar-

THE SUCCESSFUL

ried, her husband became a successful business man and she found herself thrust into a society for which, educationally, she was wholly disqualified. Realizing the situation, she began home study, secured books on language, history, literature, and studied faithfully and well, and after awhile she was one of the brightest and most charming women to be found in all of her circle. There are many women who have given up, and are failing because they had not the early chances for learning. They forget that they too might seize the many opportunities now within their grasp, which would enable them to grow and become fitted for higher and more honorable stations.

We see again the advantages of current literature. Every woman should desire to be intelligent, to keep up with the leading problems of the day. Our daily papers and magazines open the world to all. Many of our women think they must know nothing about the affairs of the day,—some think they need hardly know who are candidates for president, or governor, or anything else of that nature. They should not only know these things, but every intelligent woman should desire to be familiar with the leading affairs of the hour and to be able to converse upon them. This she may do with-

 YOUNG WOMAN

out very much work, by forming the habit of consulting the best current literature, now so easily within her reach, and she will be astonished after a short while as to how easy it is to keep up with the leading affairs.

We shall now notice for awhile something of HER NEEDS OF AN EDUCATION. She needs an education for mind discipline. Beecher said that an education would enable a woman to kindle a fire better than if she had none. It is clear to every thoughtful person that an education will help anybody. It will strengthen both mind and heart. Because she is to be a wife and have charge of household affairs, let her not think there is no necessity for education. On the contrary, there is the greatest need for the highest and best training she can possibly obtain. Then there is the forming of character. Many a helpless girl has gone down to ruin because of weakness here. Do you know that the educated women of our country seldom ever go wrong, or are seldom ensnared into the pitfalls of sin? Because of their intellectual strength they will resist temptations of the evil one, and thereby keep themselves spotless and pure as God intended that they should be. And it can be readily seen that an education is necessary for future protection in the battles of life. Many a young

in case it becomes necessary for her to make her own way in life. It serves as a heritage far better than rank, title, or money, and far better than mere position in a flimsy society. When she is educated she can make her own way, if need be, and protect herself in the battles of life that will confront her, and at the same time be independent.

Then she may obtain a practical education which need not cost her very much. Scores of young women say "I would like to have an education, but I have no opportunity." There are many such young women in our country, but if they will only stop to think, they can fit themselves with a business education that will enable them to make their own way and become independent, and not be cringing at the feet of every dude who comes along wearing a high collar and a suit of good clothes, trying to make them think that they are compelled to marry him to be protected. Instead, they can have some self independence and make their

 YOUNG WOMAN

own way. Look into the field of stenography. What possibilities are open for the young women in this line, and truly, many of our best and most efficient stenographers are women. While talking recently with a man who is editor of a large periodical, he said: "I have a stenographer who has been with me six years, and she is the best I have ever seen. I am out of the office for weeks at a time but I know everything is going all right since she is so thoroughly familiar with every detail of the work. She has become almost invaluable to the office because she has thoroughly fitted herself for the position and is filling it most efficiently, and profitably, both for herself and for the firm." And so it may be with hundreds and hundreds of others who have thought there is no remunerative place for them to fill.

Let no one understand by what has been said about women remaining single, that the very highest estimate should not be placed upon wedded life. God intended that she should enter into this sacred relation, ordinarily speaking, yet in some instances it is seen that God wills otherwise, and hence it is necessary for them to shape their life work accordingly. But the importance of education for home making cannot be overestimated. We look upon the boys of our country and say

THE SUCCESSFUL

"there are our future citizens, there are the men of tomorrow." Then we ought to look upon the girls of our homes and say "there are the wives and mothers of our land tomorrow." Not forgetting that they are the ones who will soon rule the world in large part, and exercise an influence far broader than we may think. They are to instruct the children of the commonwealth for the future; they are to stand by the husbands in the thick of the battle; they will encourage and help and sympathize in every way for the good of our country. Experience testifies that when a cause is on before the people, you will always find the good women arrayed on the right side. They will stand by the right, talk for it, encourage it and fight for it, if need be, in a way that insures victory in the end. O, the influence of educated women in a nation's homes! She needs education here to mold sentiment for good in the very largest way. Hannah Moore, to whom previous reference has been made, had this motto: "A suitable education for each, and a Christian education for all." This was the ambition of her heart. Should not that be the motto in this land, and should we not sacrifice and strive to see that our daughters are educated in a proper way? "A suitable education for each, and a Christian education for all."

YOUNG WOMAN

The average age we are told for young women to enter college is about eighteen, and the average age for graduating is about twenty-two, but a lot of folks think they must be married long before that time. Some cannot wait until eighteen, much less twenty-two. Let it be said to you, young women, and you should hear it, if you will wait until you have had an opportunity to properly educate yourself you will rarely ever be applying for a divorce after a short while when you have finally chosen a life partner. This is true because you are more apt to know enough to choose wisely, and will be strong enough to stand with him in life's conflicts and make his home what God intended you should make it. All understand that there are frequently notable exceptions to this, since the best of women are sometimes deceived by some scheming wretch, but this is not the rule. Don't be in a hurry, young woman, to get married. It may be that you can get married in a hurry, but you cannot always get unmarried in a hurry. And even if you do, there is left the sting and remorse of an unhappy union which a true woman's sensitive soul can never forget. An education, as a rule, will save our young women from an unhappy road like this. The women who have been most influential for good in

 **THE SUCCESSFUL**

public places have left an impression upon time because of their strength of soul and purity of character. Mrs. Rutherford B. Hayes refused to serve wine at public dinners, although it had long been the custom among wives in the Executive Mansion, and although court society expected it. Yet she took a determined stand against it, and her name is handed down in history today as a woman of character, far more emphasized than it would have been, or possibly could have been, if she had not manifested such strength for the right, before the whole nation.

God help and bless the good women of our land and country that they may exert their influence and power for all that is good and true and noble, educating themselves for home, store, office, school room, and public life or wherever their lot is cast, that the world may be better because they have lived and wrought in it.

II

The Young Woman and Her Circle of Friendships

"So they made him a supper there and Martha served. Mary therefore took a pound of ointment of pure nard, very precious, and annointed the feet of Jesus, and wiped his feet with her hair, and the house was filled with the odor of the ointment."—*John 12:2, 3.*

"Be not deceived, evil companionships corrupt good morals."—*I. Corinthians 15:33.*

"Life is to be fortified by many friendships. To love and to be loved, is the greatest happiness of existence."—*Sydney Smith.*

"Friendship is a sheltering tree."—*Coleridge.*

II

THE YOUNG WOMAN AND HER CIRCLE OF FRIENDSHIPS

THE first law of friendship is sincerity. That is to be the golden thread which runs through all of our best friendships. It is to have such a large place in our relations one with the other that we shall be convinced that there is no subtle deception, and no oily flattery, but beneath it all there is the strong and deep current of sincerity. If one should be placed out upon an island in the sea, having food, shelter, clothing, and all of life's luxuries, but no friends, that person would lead a life of misery. The reason is very manifest,—because there would be left out of the life one of the most vital elements of happiness, that of friendship. The touch of hearts, the communion of spirits, the helpful word, and the sympathetic look, cannot be supplied by things material. There must be that living personality of true hearts which flows out in a pure river of friendship. This world without friends would indeed be a desert place, where nothing but the winds of loneliness could be heard singing their sad notes. Of all persons

opportunity to influence for good those with whom they come in contact.

In making up this valuable circle, the first notice should be taken of the **FRIENDSHIPS IN HER OWN HOME.** Here is the starting point for almost every good thing in life. God is the author of the family and the family is set up as an institution for the well being of the country at large. From the home there is to go out an influence that will tend to brighten and help the world. There should be the strongest kind of friendship between the young woman and her parents. Sometimes parents forget that this is really necessary; nevertheless, there should be a real companionship on the part of the daughter and the parents. This is required if she is to have the highest and best guide in life, and if the parents are to be spared the pangs and heartaches afterward because of some false step or wrongdoing on her part. Many and many times parents could have saved their daughters if only they had been to them true and tried

YOUNG WOMAN

friends. Friends in whom the young woman was not afraid to confide, coming to them as her *best* friends and helpers, pouring out the innermost secrets of her heart, and asking for their advice and help that she might know how best to thread her way through the tangled maze of life.

Then, always in the home, there should exist the most beautiful friendship among brothers and sisters. There should be no disgraceful brawls in this circle to mar the family name before the community. Many times we are compelled to observe such a sad state of affairs. If there cannot be friendship here among the children, in the home circle, we are very sure there is not apt to be any strong, lasting, and worthy friendship outside of the home. The boy is to be pitied who has a bright and beautiful sister that has not found her always ready to sympathize with him and help him and guide him in his life affairs. Then pity for the sister who has not found her brother a companion and helper, one who is such a true friend that he will constantly throw about her the arm of protection in the most trying scenes she is called upon to enter. It is a very cruel kind of a young man who will not manifest an affectionate friendship for his sister, and in such a way that the world

THE SUCCESSFUL

will in no wise be mistaken as to his affection for her. Young women should prize the brother's friendship highly, and should cultivate it constantly. They should delight to let the world know of one who is a true friend and will stand by them in times of stress when perhaps others would turn away.

We might look again with reference to the family relationships outside of the immediate home. There ought to be the very best friendship existing between young women and their kinspeople. We know that very often privileges are abused here; they sometimes think because of the tie of blood that they may take advantage one of the other in various ways. Still there should exist the truest and most beautiful friendship possible.

In discussing friendships made in the home we should not forget those who come into it as visitors. They will bring to us much that is good and helpful from the outside world, and we should endeavor not only to be polite to them but also to cultivate them and win them as friends. We should endeavor to form such a friendly relationship with them that when they go out again into the world they will exercise their influence so as to enlarge the sphere of the life which they have found and thus make it better.

YOUNG WOMAN

Those who have read the story of Madame de Maintenon, last wife of Louis XIV of France, have learned that she was a woman of very commonplace station in her early days. Even so poor that she was sent out into the fields to tend the flocks, look after the poultry, and engage in the most menial services from day to day. But because of her winning nature, her true heart and great intellect, she commanded the respect of those who came in contact with her in her home. They carried out into the world news of what they had discovered, and thus it went on from time to time until this poor girl had a great many influential friends, and she finally occupied the highest place of any woman in France. This was brought about because she had cultivated the friendship of those who came into her humble life, while they carried back to the world what they had found, making it realize that they had discovered a great soul. She later occupied the palace and held sway over this monarch for a period of years as no other woman had ever done in all of his career.

Then looking again into the home we should not forget the importance of the friendship that should exist between the young woman and the servants. Queen Victoria said "a good servant is a good friend," and that prin-

in your homes. This friendship should
as is in keeping, of course, with the
that each is to occupy, but there should
iendship that will be helpful to the
s. This may be shown in the matter
ation and religion, since here is offered
pportunity to accomplish real and last-
d. Many and many times servants have
helpfulness in homes where they had
labor, that brought them into true re-
ip with God; therefore, there should
right kind of friendship on the part of
ing woman with the servants in her

shall consider now HER FRIEND-
AMONG THE MEMBERS OF HER
SEX. In the early days of girlhood
young woman should desire to have a
irele of friends among girls of her own
iends in whom she delights and who
found helpful and sympathetic as she
long the happy pathway of girlhood.
is the woman who does not even yet
ick with delight to her girlhood days
ink of their friendships, with joy and
less? In school days chums are to be
d about you. They will serve to give
in the task of education and help you

 YOUNG WOMAN

as together you study and recite, as hand in hand you go out and gather wild flowers, as secretly you talk and plan for the great future. These friendships some might say are hardly worth our notice, and yet they are some of the brightest flowers that ever blossomed in the lives of young women.

Going a step further and looking into college life, we find in this place she is to have friendships that will mean much to her in after years, because college ties are very apt to be the strongest links which friendship forges. This is true in the history of both men and women. College friendships are those that last through the years, since they have been made at a time when the lives are formative. These friendships will cement so solidly that time rarely ever causes them to crumble and decay. They will last on and on, and you later look with fondness here and yonder to some prominent woman, remembering the days you toiled together, and noting anew the brilliant scene when you stood before the president of the school and received your diplomas, as an honorable reward for weeks and years of study and planning side by side. You should endeavor to gather about you here not only congenial companions, but intellectual companions as well. They will prove to be a great

THE SUCCESSFUL

bulwark of strength for the battle that you will be in, and for the ceaseless struggle that you will have while endeavoring to make your own way with renown and honor as a true woman. You will then come home with an honor-crowned brow, not only because you have mastered the prescribed course, but have also gathered about you friends who will ever prove helpful. You should have here associates that are noble and true, and who will bring into your life thoughts that are as beautiful as the very thoughts of God. Let them be persons whose lives are chaste and pure and whose works are a charm and a joy all along as together you go. Such friends will continually enrich your life and make it shine forth with a halo of heavenly glory.

We come now to consider the question of HER FRIENDSHIPS AMONG MEMBERS OF THE OPPOSITE SEX. Here it is necessary, as well in what we have already discussed, for the best thinking and the most serious planning on the part of young women. The degree of friendships in this direction may vary to some extent and ought to vary. Yet there is no real reason why a young woman should not have friendships among members of the opposite sex, when no thoughts of the conjugal relation exist. There is no reason why there

YOUNG WOMAN

should not be such friendships among members of the opposite sex, that will be helpful. As to the number of these friendships, it may differ; some may say that the world scorns the idea of a young woman having a large circle of friends among young men. But we plead for a large circle of friendships here. Many young women, as beautiful as God could make them, have had the friendship and the utmost respect of a large circle of young men, and that without any unholy jealousies being aroused. This was made possible because the young men realized that such women were not flirts, but rather pure hearts, and true lives. The right sort of young women will always be helpful, giving courage and inspiration to the lives of the right sort of young men. We call to mind now an experience in other days, where a young woman proved to be one of the truest and best friends and advisers in the life of a young man who had become discouraged. The thought of any other relation than that of true friendship never came into the mind of either, but the life of the young man was spurred up and on to things that were high and elevating. Later in life his efforts were crowned with success, and largely because this friendship had existed. The time came when these lives were separated and no misunder-

 **THE SUCCESSFUL**

standing ever arose, since nothing other than true friendship was intended from the first. There can be no just reason why friendships like this should not exist. Then it will give the young woman another advantage; it will keep her from becoming so secluded as to narrow her vision of life and corner it off, from the world for a period of years. Instances are numerous where this has been done by unfaithful young men who later have turned away from her, and she is left almost alone because she allowed herself to become secluded with but few friendships. Young women, this is one of the most important points in your career. Let your circle of friendships be such that you may choose wisely and well when it comes to the matter of a life partner. Do not allow a rigid seclusion with some *one* through a period of years to keep you from making other friends. Most young men do not want to marry a young woman who can command the friendship of only one or two persons.

As to the kind of friends, she should note well the type of character, choosing only friends of the opposite sex who are of the noblest character. Let the world once know our associates and it knows us, because judgment is rendered largely by the character of our daily companions. No young woman who

YOUNG WOMAN

cares anything for herself can afford to have friendships among members of the opposite sex who do not give every evidence of the truest and noblest lives. Turn away from those whose lives are corrupt and whose reputations are bad, as you would from a poisonous serpent. Leave them alone, because they mean nothing but to drag you down into sin, they mean nothing except to ruin your character, destroy your beautiful life and deprive you henceforth from standing as a pure woman among pure women, filling a noble place in the service of Almighty God. You should think seriously here, and be willing, young woman, to hear the wise words of true parents. They will do only that for you which is intended to be helpful and good, and will not advise merely that they may cross your wishes. With true parents advice is given only that they may prove themselves true helpers and faithful friends. Then again, young woman, avoid the idler, from the mere street corner loafers to the kid glove dude and spendthrift; let him have no place in your circle of friendships, save as it might be in your ability to help him, but be very careful lest he prove a dead weight and the relationship become disastrous. Look not down, young woman, for your circle of friendships. Look up and don't seek beneath

an outcast who has neither character nor
ation. Seek those who come from our
homes and have proven by their lives and
act that they are worthy of your respect,
athy, and comradeship.

e wish now to think of HER FRIEND-
S IN THE LITERARY WORLD. May
meone would say there is no place or
here for talk about friendships in the life
e ordinary young woman, but there is a
large place. Every young woman should
e to have some literary friends. She
ld desire to have those of the best reputa-
remembering that the literary air does
lways mean character. She is to seek the
 of those whose companionship will be
 helpful and inspire her to the highest
ing and noblest living. There are the
dships of literary clubs; young women
have their literary clubs conducted in such
anner that they will be worth much to
, both in making friends and in opening up
 of usefulness which they could not other-
have.

rning aside from persons, let us talk just
ment about your friendships among the
s. A book as a friend, you say? Yes.
 of the best friends many young women
had were found among good books. Books

YOUNG WOMAN

that opened to them the world, that inspired their thoughts to higher and more serious thinking and living, and really caused them to come to themselves. She should endeavor to secure those books that will arouse in her mind thoughts of usefulness, and that will really make her life count for something. Charles Dudley Warner said "An underbred book is worse than any possible epidemic." So many lives are really ruined by trashy literature which engages the mind constantly. Have you stopped to think when you are reading a book that you are hearing someone speak to your mind and heart, and that it is just as wrong, and just as hurtful to read a trashy book from a disreputable author as it is to talk and associate with, in person, a disreputable character? This is true because you are taking in the very thought and life of another person when you are reading his book. Fichte once said, when reading a blood-curdling novel, "This will never do; I get too much excited over it. I cannot study so well afterwards, so here it goes," throwing the book into the river, not longer willing to waste his time with such trashy stuff. Then her selections of books ought to be such that will arouse in her aspirations to achieve a successful place in the world, whether it be in some humble home or

 **THE SUCCESSFUL**

whether it be in public station. Ruskin has said "The best romance becomes dangerous if by its excitement it renders ordinary courses of life uninteresting and creates a morbid thirst for acquaintances in scenes which we shall never be called to enter." There is room here for honest thinking on your part. Show us the kind of books the young woman is reading and we will tell you much as to the true nature of her aspirations in life, and something about her circle of friendships, for soon she endeavors to make book-characters, real characters. And then finally, she should read only those books that will bring before her the world of the past and of the present in its true relationship with men and affairs. Then let her find her place in the great throng where she may be most helpful in the service of humanity, and where she may spend her life to the greatest advantage. She is well fitted at this point to gather about her a circle of friends that will be the most helpful, and at the same time enable her to be most helpful to them. How beautiful is friendship! Nothing will take the place of it in all the world. It is thrilling music in our lives. It is sweet aroma from the garden of true companionship. It is a receptacle into which we can pour our bitterest sorrows, and bring them forth again tempered and

 ## YOUNG WOMAN

sweetened by the dew of sympathy. It is the golden tie that binds heart to heart, and a bright shining emblem of the friendship that is to exist in the beautiful land beyond.

Young woman, in all of your friendships forget not Him who liberated you, who loves you and gave Himself for you. He it was who has made it possible for you to occupy the queenly place in life that you occupy today. To Him be faithful and true, gather around Him as did those faithful women of old, and let Him be the truest and best friend in your life. Look forward to the day when not only His face shall shine upon you in this world, but to the time when He shall open the Heavenly portals to you at last and you shall enter into His eternal rest, there to enjoy the friendship of Him forevermore.

III

The Young Woman Making Her Own Way in the World

"And Ruth, the Moabitess, said unto Naomi, Let me now go to the field and glean among the ears of grain after him in whose sight I shall find favor. And she said unto her, Go, my daughter."—Ruth 2:2.

"Nature fits all her children with something to do."—Lowell.

*"Thus I steer my bark, and sail,
On even keel, with gentle gale."*
—*Green.*

III

THE YOUNG WOMAN MAKING HER OWN WAY IN THE WORLD

ONE cannot enter into the discussion of a theme like this without being deeply impressed as to its great importance. When we look out into the commercial world in all of its departments of life today and behold the great army of young women who are making their own way, we very readily concede that this is a practical theme. This is no longer theory; it is now fact. When we discuss it we are reminded of the contrast of the ideas that prevail now, with the ideas that prevailed in the past. There was a time not very far away when a young woman's only outlook for the future was matrimony, and if she failed in this she was to be regarded as one of the unfortunates in life. Very happily that day has largely passed and is rapidly passing forever.

In considering this theme we shall look first at THE NECESSITY OF HER MAKING HER OWN WAY IN THE WORLD. It often happens now that such necessity does exist with large numbers of young women. The necessity comes very frequently because of circum-

...ices at home over which they have no con... . There are hundreds, yea thousands in ...land, to say nothing about the great armies ...young women in other lands, that are wholly ...endent very early in life upon their own ...orts to live. Since this is true it is quite ...essary for that part of the world which is ...a position to help them to be thoroughly ...quainted with the situation. It is also necessary that the young women themselves should ...fully aroused to the great fact that the ...rld wants women who are capable and com-...ent to fill the positions open to them.

While informing ourselves upon this subject ...have been struck with the notoriety of a ...mber of noble women in other days who ...rted from the humblest homes. Because of ...ir industry, their noble character and ster-...g worth, they won their way to places of ...nor and renown as well as amply supporting ...emselves, and in many instances others who ...re dependent upon them. Such was the ...perience of Mary Lyon who started in life ...m the humblest walk. Her mother died ...en she was a mere child, and at the age of ...irteen for Mary, the father married again, ...d she was left to keep house for a brother. ...allowed her the great sum of one dollar ...r week to keep house for him, and out of this

meagre amount she yet found out how she could save to buy books and thereby fit herself for a higher position in life. When she was eighteen years of age, her brother married and left her entirely alone in the world, and she was thrown upon her own resources. She began teaching for about seventy-five cents per week, yet saved enough to take a course in school herself. After she went through the first term her money was gone, but she had won honor in the eyes of her teachers; they had been struck with her great mind, and offered her free tuition for another term, but she did not have money to pay her board. This difficulty was solved, however, by selling the small articles she had, such as a bed, some pieces of linen, etc., to a boarding house keeper, which enabled her to remain another term in school. Her heart was set upon establishing a school that she might fit other young women for better advantages to serve in life than she had been able to enjoy. She started out almost as a pioneer in establishing schools for young women. She was met with every discouragement, but persevered until after awhile her dream was realized. Mount Holyoke College of Massachusetts was established and she was its principal for a number of years. From that school thousands of young women have gone out better fitted for

 **THE SUCCESSFUL**

the struggles of life. And why? Because it was founded upon great heart principles. It was guided by a spirit that knew no failure, and had embodied a vision for usefulness as large as the world itself.

Citation could be made to a number of others were it necessary in the discussion of this theme. Many of us have been thrilled again and again with the names of great women that adorn the pages of history today because they developed themselves by battling in life to the places which they filled so honorably and so worthily. Let us have the greatest respect for those lives that are thrown out upon the world to shift for themselves. Look not at them with a scornful eye, but rather think of them with a desire to help and lift up, so as to enable them to occupy a worthy place in life's broad field.

There are many young women who go out into the world to make their own way merely because of their capabilities and peculiar fitness for certain kinds of work. Their education and general training have been such that they are admirably fitted for a place of usefulness. They are not content at sitting idly down from day to day in a home where they might be cared for comfortably, perhaps, when there is an opportunity to go into the arena of

YOUNG WOMAN

life and make their own way. All honor to a woman who desires to utilize her powers, and at the same time fill a place where she may do great good.

Then again we see in that class, a large army of women who are fired by the conviction that they should lead a life of usefulness by fulfilling a certain mission. They not only make a living for themselves, but larger still, they use their influence to help others, and create for them a life-vision of usefulness which they could not have but for these leaders who blaze the way. Here is, indeed, manifested the true missionary spirit when they sacrifice to fill a place which will bless humanity at large. They go out into the world not for self, but for others, thinking not mainly of their own welfare, but thinking at the same time and more largely, too, of the blessings their lives will shower on the thousands who come into touch with them.

Now let us look at the **VARIOUS AVENUES OPEN FOR YOUNG WOMEN AT THE PRESENT DAY.** There are far more opportunities now than there have ever been at any other time. In the professional world the school room is open to them as never before; so much so that in fact they are crowding out the men almost entirely. The women now have charge

THE SUCCESSFUL

of our schools very largely, everywhere you go, not only as teachers of grades, but they are occupying the chair of principal and superintendent of schools. In some places there are lady superintendents of entire counties, which shows that this important field is today open to them more than ever. None need be sorry that this is true; when you think of their lives and measure their character, you note that they are fitted to fill these important places. As a general thing this noble army of women have the very best character and are occupying a place of honor and respect that any woman might be proud to occupy. Then her patience fits her admirably for this work. How painstaking and careful must a true teacher be, and we do not find the grace of patience displayed more prominently on the part of any persons than on the part of our women, who are molding the character and lives of our children as they preside over them in the schoolroom. Truly it may be said that a large and important place is found here for capable and ambitious young women.

We see also that many other avenues are open to her in the professional world. Medicine is inviting her services as at no other time. Especially is this true in the department of skillful nursing. She is now gliding through

YOUNG WOMAN

the hospitals of our cities, going into the homes of the sick among private citizens as nurse, and giving the tenderest ministrations and offering the greatest help that can possibly come to the suffering. What a large field is here open to the young woman. What a great opportunity is there for her in this direction. Many women are going into the profession of law and are occupying in some places of our country positions of importance in this profession. We shall not attempt to discuss at length this particular phase of opportunity, but merely say that the practice of law is open to you. We note again how prominent she has been and is becoming in music and art. Many of the best musicians of this and of other lands are now found among women. We can see how readily and how naturally she takes to this art and how patiently and persistently she presses forward until she gains renown as well as a handsome income by her perseverence in this sphere. And in the realm of art she is not absent, but is beginning to rank with the renowned painters and sculptors, showing the world that she has talent for this work which will remunerate her labors and bring her fame.

Then turning to the large offices in our commercial emporiums young women are found in great throngs who are satisfactorily filling

 **THE SUCCESSFUL**

their places and more than rendering value received to their employers. They are filling some of the most important positions in the offices of our country, both in commercial and political pursuits; and how astonishing it has become that they have developed such talent in this direction. Look at our stenographers and you will find among this great army of workers some of the most efficient in the entire profession are women, and under almost all circumstances they can be relied upon for the best and speediest work required. Statistics reveal the fact that large numbers of them can be found who are able to take any kind of dictation that any other stenographer can take, and take it most accurately, and be relied upon to reproduce their notes, giving exactly what was spoken. A recent and well written article on this subject enumerated some of the particular qualifications of the most successful women stenographers; it spoke of the characteristics of the most efficient ones, such as promptness, industry, proper dress for the office, etc. They learn how to dress plainly and how to live lives that are modest and unassuming and do work that the gaudily dressed girl cannot do. Among commercial men, excessive dressing, and the queenly air of the dime novel type, usually mean poor service, and hence poor pay;

YOUNG WOMAN

while the neat and plainly dressed girl means efficient service and good wages.

Many of the best bookkeepers today are women, serving as competent accountants; they are skilful, accurate, rapid, and trusted in all commercial transactions. You will find them at many desks in our business establishments throughout the country. They are also becoming telegraphers and sitting at the keys causing the news to flash like lightning across the land, and proving themselves equal in skill and accuracy with men in telegraphic work, both in railroad and commercial service. Again they are found as newspaper reporters; many of them going here and yonder gathering news for the press, and writing it up in the most attractive fashion, to the delight of a reading public.

Let us now turn to the consideration of woman's work in the great department stores of the cities. Here young women are found in large numbers. In nearly every department they are handling the situation to the complete satisfaction of all parties concerned. If they were not doing this we would not find them there waiting upon the trade, as well and in many cases even better, than men. When we speak of this particular part of the woman's life it is wished that a word might be said

which would go into the ears of every employer in our department stores in all of this land and country. There is no place where women are rendering more valuable service than here, and perhaps in our large department stores in great cities there is no place where they are worse treated by many employers. When this is said reference is made not only to the hours of service, but to the demands that are made upon them when you consider the meagre wages they usually receive. In some of these great department stores the character of young women is tried with as much severity as in most any other walk of life. This is made so because of what is expected of them as to their dress and general appearance before the public, and of persons often wholly dependent upon them in their homes for existence. Here their character is severely tried, and too many times to the breaking point, that too, largely because those in charge are not willing to give them a living wage, but prefer instead to pile up blood money to their own account. This is one of the most serious problems we have to confront today, and one that calls for a speedy remedy on the part of those who would see justice done to this noble army of women who are being made to suffer.

Then again the young woman fills an impor-

YOUNG WOMAN

tant place at the cash register: how skilful she becomes here. Watch her in the crowded places in any great city as she hands out change almost like the working of an automatic machine. Nothing but patience, skill and close application can accomplish such achievements. And who is proving more efficient in this exceedingly important position than woman? Men are checked up short in their cash a dozen times to a woman's one.

Now there are **SOME SPECIAL WARNINGS** that should be considered in the study of this subject. One of the surest signs of wisdom is for persons to note the danger points along life's roads, so as to avoid them. This is doubly true of woman, as her mistakes are far more serious in the world's eye than the mistakes of men. It is necessary for her to guard her character stringently when she is thrown out upon her own resources. There are hundreds and thousands of fiendish wretches who will lie in wait to destroy her very life. On the other hand, let us frankly say that hundreds of good people are throwing about her an environment of protection. But it is necessary for her to guard her own character, with a caution such as no one else can and will guard it, since temptation will seek her at almost every turn in life's way.

She should not allow the home ties t
severed any more than possible, but sh
always endeavor to keep in her heart a
pathy and love for the home, for the fa
fireside. It is often hard, in a way at least
her to do this, but if she will think much a
this line it will save her many a time v
everything else has failed. It will go fa
wards keeping in her mind the great fact
God intended that she should be the h
maker, and should give the home her pr
ence when the right opportunity is offered.
should be willing to come out of comme
life at the proper time and take her plac
queen of the home. Just here perhaps son
our women make a serious mistake. V
they know what it means to become :
pendent, there may be a strong inclinatic
turn away from the idea of taking upon t
selves the responsibility of a home.
again, it is necessary for her to think seri(
and carefully. To be sure it is much b
for her to make her own way in the world
for her to marry some worthless scamp v
she would have to support. But let it ev
kept in mind, that God intended, ordin:
that her place should be in the home. 1
she will find her throne, and there she w
enabled to serve the world in a far better

 YOUNG WOMAN

as a rule, than she can possibly serve it in any other place.

Finally let it be noted that she is not to forget her best and truest friend, Jesus of Nazareth. God has given to her a liberty that she never enjoyed before and never could have enjoyed in all the earth if Christ had not come to take away the shackles of bondage that were making her man's slave. Let it here be said in a word of commendation that no class of persons can be cited who should have the friendship of mankind more heartily than this noble army of toiling young women. Taking them with their struggles, difficulties, and constant temptations, none are more deserving of the hearty hand of help and sympathy than they.

Take our churches throughout the country generally, and you will not find any persons more loyal to them than the young women who are thrown out upon the world to make their own way. In great liberality do they come with their gifts and place them upon the altar of God. When you hear someone say that all of these young women are going to the bad, you can nail it down as a lie, and you can say also that many of the best wives this world has ever seen have come from this class of young women. And you can say again that the churches of Jesus Christ have found scores

and hundreds and thousands of most loyal supporters from this band of young women. They give of their means that they have earned by their skill, exercised in honest toil, as many others fail to do who are able to give dollars where these are able to give only dimes. We should have nothing but words of good cheer and highest commendation for the vast army of young women who are thrown out upon their own resources in life's battles.

In a closing word we would address parents, and say forget not that your daughter may be thrown out upon the world after you are gone. Hence it becomes you to fit her as far as you are able for life's duties, by education and everything that will give her power. Should the necessity arise for her to earn her own way she can then do so most creditably and honorably. Thereby you will guard and protect her as you could not with mere social standing, or dollars, or political influence. You give her a stability by education that will enable her to fill a place somewhere in life's broad field, such as you would not be ashamed of could you look back from the grave and see her. God's choicest blessing be upon the vast army of young women who go out into the world to make their own way.

IV

The Young Woman and Her Influence

*"Grace is deceitful, and beauty is vai[n]
woman that feareth the Lord shall be p[raised]."
—Proverbs 31:30.*

*"The society of women is the found[ation of]
good manners."—Goethe.*

*"The woman who is resolved to be r[espected]
can make herself so even amidst an [army of]
soldiers."—Cervantes.*

IV

THE YOUNG WOMAN AND HER INFLUENCE

FEW themes are more vital to the young womanhood of our country than this one. When we speak of influence we are readily reminded that each and everyone has an influence of some kind. It is true that the influence of certain ones is larger and counts for more than the influence of others. Yet there has never been a life so insignificant, and considered so worthless by the world, that it was devoid entirely of influence in some degree. We have heard often the old illustration, that if you take a mere pebble and drop it into the sea it will start waves circling out all around it, and that these waves never stop until they break upon the shore perhaps thousands of miles away. While they are not long perceptible to the natural eye, and while no great power is being manifested, at the same time the effect is going on, and on. So it is with every life that God had dropped into the great sea of time. Each life has its power and its influence, and is telling upon the lives of yet other persons with whom it comes into touch.

It should be the sincere and earnest
of every man and woman to so live tl
influence cast is that which will be th
best. Let it be such that it will enricl
lives, so that they may think of yoı
helper. Your influence in the lives of
is either a weight that drags them do
wings that lift them up. Influence may
exercised as to prove a demon of destr
or an angel of light.

We know of no class of persons whos
are so influential and really count for ε
much, as the lives of young women.
his creative work chose to make maı
and to make woman nèxt, but in doiı
he made her the flower of his creatio
made her the most beautiful, the most
ential of the two by far, and intended tl
life should brighten and sweeten the
man as together they were to go in the
Her influence is to be such that it reael
toward God, and toward all that is go
stands for righteousness and truth and
refining power that far outstrips the iı
of man.

We shall think together in the dis
of this important subject, primarily
FIRST STEP IN HER INFLUENCE.
to begin in her own home, by prope

 YOUNG WOMAN

training. As to her sex, the young woman, or rather the girl in the home, ought to be taught that to be a woman in the high and true sense of the term is to be the noblest and best creature beneath the stars of God. Sometimes we hear it said that the baby girl is not welcomed by parents, that the girl's life is not counted for much; that people are disappointed because the girl comes into the home. Parents should teach the girl child that God made her thus and that he created her for usefulness in his great domain. She should be taught that she is to fill a mission that is heaven born, and that she is to lead a life that is holy and righteous, and one which will make the world brighter and sweeter and better because she has been brought into it. If this were done more than it is, there would be a premium placed upon the women of our land by many persons today, who rather sneer at the idea of being a woman, or of a woman really having any influence that is to count for very much, or that is worthy the strength of a great life. Instruction at this point should be as to the womanly graces,—her conduct and all should be started properly here; so that later when out in the world, wherever her lot is cast, she will know how to conduct herself as a woman who has been instructed in the chief charms

 **THE SUCCESSFUL**

of womanhood. She will then be able
out the divine plan in life and perform
worthy of such a plan.

Going a step further we can see
strength of her influence is to be cast
by proper education. Her education
teach her what it really means to b(
world and to show to the world w]
womanhood is. It should enable her
that womanhood does not mean t
"flounces" or to display dry goods an(
jewelry, and to pose for the evil gaze
minded men; but on the contrary, that
hood means to fill the very highest, t
best, and the very largest place that a
fill. In addition to that, there is to]
instruction that will reveal to her
worthy life really is, and the things f(
it should stand. Sometimes we are m
very much mistaken in this direction;
those who have the idea that beauty a
accomplishments are the only things
which count for real worth and are
true passports into life. But the
woman should be taught that her usefu
place in life, is to be measured by the
of her heart, the greatness of her soul
purity and sweetness of her character
this estimate is placed upon life by t]

YOUNG WOMAN

are instructing and guiding her, and when this estimate is seen and accepted by the young women themselves, then it is that they will go out into the world with an influence, and with a power that far outstrips anything that they have ever before known. And then it is that the world at large will begin to feel the pulsating life of pure, true and noble womanhood as never before felt by it. We plead for the young woman to have the best chance, that she may fit herself to cast an influence over all within her circle, that is good and true and holy.

Further let us discuss **THE POWER OF HER INFLUENCE**. In doing this we shall note first the power of her influence for evil. You have often heard it said that when a person is really evil, or when a life has sure enough gone to the very depths of degradation, that there is nothing which becomes so very low or so fearfully repulsive as the life of a woman. It may truly be said that she is either the best thing or the worst thing in all the earth. Her influence for evil when the life is wrongly guided cannot be measured by our finite minds. Observe how her influence for evil is shown over members of her own sex. Those who have taken the pains to look into the causes of the evils of young women in great

cities, find in numerous instances
women are employed to decoy and
younger members of their sex, a
lead them into sin. These words
said, and they should be thrown ou
ing to the young women who read
and to the older ones as well, whose
influence the lives of other memb
sex. We read in the word of God
bels, of the Sapphiras, and of the
women there mentioned, but their
always condemned in strong lang
history reveals to us the lives of n
who have filled important place
been raised to where they could ha
an influence of wondrous power fo
they chose to so live as to degrad
lives they touched. A bad woman
power may influence for evil a wh
nation. Those who have read th
the French Revolution have been
the fact that in the Court of Fr
great number of women whose ir
for the worst forms of evil. Such
places tended to hurry the natio
awful scenes so soon to be enacted
horrified the whole civilized worl

Now that we have discussed wc
ence for evil first, let us turn aw

disagreeable phase of the subject and think last of the better side, which is far more pleasant. In both directions it is readily seen how her influence has counted, and how it continues to count every day. In morality she is the balance wheel of every community; each community is just about as moral as the women of that community make it. And so, good women, you have within your power the possibility of making your community a moral community, if you will exert the influence you may exert for good, working from the home outward. Others will soon know that there are women within their realm who love purity and righteousness, and soon their power for good will be felt and known, and will serve nobly in the community life. Holy Writ speaks far oftener of good women than it does of bad women. We have all heard from our earliest years of the Sarahs, the Rebekahs, the Rachels and the Marys. History is also full of the names of great and good women, but we shall discuss them more fully under the head of The Young Woman in Public Life.

Note also her influence in spiritual things. She might be called the spiritual thermometer of the home. As a rule the home is just about as religious as the woman makes it. Go into the home of a godly woman, a woman whose

heart, life and very soul are bound
spiritual things, and you find a home
everyone who comes within the range of
fluence will know about the Lord God, a
be made to feel the power of a godly life
very atmosphere of heaven just natural
rounds it and goes out on every hand.
is a spiritual glow that is manifest all a
and the lives which come into contac
that home are compelled to feel the wo
power of the noble and godly life
Thinking of matters moral and spiritua
observed often that our young women
as particular as they might be, and a
should be, about their young men comp
Some young women allow themselves to
foolish as to think they must never refu
companionship of any young men wh
to go with them, lest they might not ha
portunity for companionship at all. In
the opposite is true. Every young man
worthy the companionships of a tru
wants a young woman who places th
highest estimate upon morality and puri
will look upon her as a premium an
pride when she gains for herself the n
being careful as to her associates among
men, demanding of them correctness
and a stainless character before they m

YOUNG WOMAN

enjoy her society. Young woman, don't be afraid just here; assert yourself, in the right way of course, but let it be understood fully that you yourself place a premium upon lives that are noble and true, and that the young man's conduct must be good if he is ever to have your companionship in any capacity, save merely to offer the hand of help when there is a real cry of distress.

Finally, let us note **THE AVENUES OF HER INFLUENCE.** This carries us back to her own family circle, where first her influence is exercised. Many a hard-hearted and rugged father has been led into the saving knowledge of the Son of God by a daughter who had learned early in life to love the Saviour. Again and again have we noted instances of this kind. It is very hard for a father to long resist the pleading of a pure and sweet young woman who is his own flesh and blood, beseeching him to turn away from the walks of sin and seek a place in the kingdom of the Lord. A real case to illustrate this is cited: A father had the habit of taking his children to church and leaving them at the door, then going himself to spend the day in sin. When he placed his little girl down at the church door one Sabbath morning, she threw her arms about his neck and held on, and with tears in her eyes, she

THE SUCCESSFUL

told him how he was bringing sorrow and misery into the home when he came back intoxicated, and how mother and the children were afraid of him while he was in that condition. This tender, yet true statement was too much for him; it melted his heart and served to lead him into a true knowledge and tender love of the Saviour. It was the beginning of an influence that was to be powerful among his companions, and to count for much in leading them into the kingdom of God. This same thing is repeated again and again by the young women of our land when they really reach the point where they surrender their own lives fully and unreservedly to Jesus Christ.

The next place where she casts a wonderful influence is in the social circles of our country. Social circles are very much what the young women make them. There should be no thirsting desire on her part to shine as a glittering star in the sky of much so called society, as in many places we have it today. There is something which is far better than that. As a rule, the life which will attract the most attention in what is commonly called the social circle, is the one that has the most time to throw away, the most finery to display on various occasions, and the most leisure for idle and hurtful gossip. That is about the kind of life a

YOUNG WOMAN

woman is expected to lead in the fashionable world if she is ever to become a star in its sky.

Then again, we see how her influence counts in the church of the living God. Here her influence is more powerful than the influence of any other company of persons to be found. When you go into the churches today you find in them all a band of women who stand by God Almighty's work when the men have grown tired and have become indifferent and allowed themselves to turn away. Yet the women, noble and true, with their hearts bound up in the religion of our Lord, are the last to leave the cross and the first to reach the tomb. After the world has said the church is dead and ready to be buried, you will find them lingering about the corpse and pleading the promise of the resurrection; and you will find that God has given them the power to resurrect dead churches. It may be said safely and truly to you, young women, that you cannot find a place where your influence is worth more than in the Kingdom of God. There you may exert an influence that will tell in your home, that will tell in society, that will tell in the world at large, and that will tell on and on until eternity itself shall have come. God alone, who keeps the record, knows how much your life will count for his glory when rightly used. We

cannot overestimate the importance of your exercising the right influence at all times; nor can we overestimate the power of such influence. One of the things that should cheer us most is that when we look about everywhere, we see great armies of noble and true women coming from Christian homes, and being educated in Christian colleges. They go out into the world to let their trained lives work within its society, never stopping until the whole lump is leavened for good, for righteousness, for purity, and for truth. Without doubt the noonday of God's love is being ushered in through their influence.

It has already been said that what we need in our country today is educated mothers. Let us elaborate by saying these must be educated and Christian mothers who preside over the homes of our land and rear the children of coming generations. Then the children of the future will go out with an educated Christian mother's blessing and benediction. They will go out into the great world wearing a crown of honor that will shine with a never failing lustre wherever their lot is cast, and that will have for its chief jewel a Christian mother's love.

V

The Young Woman and Her Affections

"And Ruth said: Entreat me not to leave thee, and to return from following after thee; for whither thou goest, I will go; and where thou lodgest, I will lodge; thy people shall be my people, and thy God my God; where thou diest, will I die, and there will I be buried, the Lord do so to me, and more also, if aught but death part thee and me."—*Ruth 16:17.*

"Love never faileth."—*I. Corinthians 13:8.*

"Alas! the love of woman! it is known
To be a lovely and a fearful thing."
—*Byron.*

"And when a woman says she loves a man,
The man must hear her, though he love her not."
—*E. B. Browning.*

V

THE YOUNG WOMAN AND HER AFFECTIONS

LOVE has ever inspired the poet. It has charmed the orator. It has aroused the skill of the painter. And it has had more to do with the happiness, as well as with the misery, of human hearts than any other one thing in all the world. When we think of the affection of woman we think of it as the perfume of the rose, as the well spring of happiness, as the glittering jewel of life, and as the bond of union between true souls. Again, as the roseate dawn of life, as the golden light of noon, and as the lingering twilight of closing day. So highly important is it that it ought to engage the most serious thought of each and everyone, of the sage, the professional man, the business man, the peasant and the man of the palace. This great question should be treated with such seriousness that there might come from it those things which really have to do with making happy the human heart.

In treating this theme one cannot do better than to notice first **THE NATURE OF WOMAN'S AFFECTIONS**. Her affections are

Here is also the very center of her ambition; her whole soul is embarked in the traffic of affection, and if lost the heart becomes bankrupt. As food is necessary for the body, so to her is affection necessary for sustenance of the heart. It gives and strengthens character, and here, dear friends, is that which should be noted with great seriousness on your part. Someone has very well said that "The virtuous woman says no; the passionate woman says yes; the capricious woman, yes and no; and the coquette says neither yes or no." It is further said that "The coquette is a rose from whom every lover plucks a leaf, leaving nothing but the thorn for her future husband."

 YOUNG WOMAN

This is often true in the experience of the world, and it is so frequently the case that it ought to engage the serious and honest thinking of every right-minded woman. True heart love gives not only character but it gives sweetness also. A woman's life without affection is an odorless flower, a tasteless fruit, an insipid nothingness.

We might also think upon this theme with reference to the OBJECTS OF HER AFFECTION, and in so doing let us note the beginning, or the affection as first it dawns. It manifests itself in the nursery; the little life lavishes love upon her dolls and pets. Her numerous doll children have her affection, and her pets have her warmest and most sympathetic care. This is nothing more than the born instinct of love in the woman's heart. Again, it invests itself in the days of dreamy girlhood. Oftentimes it happens that the young girl imagines herself in love when she does not so much as know the outer edge of its deep meaning. It does not hurt much to dream along this line, as a rule, yet there are times when mere idle dreaming leads away from the path of virtue and purity.

But let us notice especially something of the affection when Cupid's dart first strikes the heart. Someone has said that Cupid has had

THE SUCCESSFUL

his innings from the cave dweller's t:
on in every age and condition of li
winged darts fly into the luxurious
and find their way into the humblest
homes on the hillside. In every l:
clime they find their way into th
of the rich and of the poor. God h;
dained that this should be so. In her
experience the young woman will hid
away within the solitude of her own
and revel in a sea of glory, almost afra
knowledge to herself the new foun
Here she dreams of valleys scented w
and sparkling with gushing founta
looks out upon mountains of joy rea
the very heavens, in the hours when
dart has first pierced her heart. A
awhile she will confide in a companior
gether they repaint the petals of Ede

How happy are these days, how gol
moments, how glad these hours, how
this time in the life of a young wom
how serious, and how important in
And let us here say, beloved friends,
the tact and skill of the mother shor
into the circle of the daughter's life.
the mother who would strive to des
budding flower in the life of her dat
who would cause it to wither and die

YOUNG WOMAN

to turn her heart away from some young man, worthy and upright in the path of God, to some sin besotted youngster who may perchance inherit a fortune that he never helped to make, and which may fly away in a few short months to leave them in misery and sadness the rest of their days. Young woman, think deeply just here. It is not every man who comes along with the jingle of golden coin that is able to make you happy; it is not every mansion that might swing open its portals to you, that will give to you the real joy of home which your heart craves. Rather may it be that someone who occupies a more modest place in life as the world chooses to say, can make you happier and do more for you, if his heart and soul are bound up in God, and if he be upright in the walks of life.

We shall notice in the last instance something of the **POWER OF HER AFFECTIONS**. This is manifested in the home, where the affection of woman is the ministering spirit. It is the guardian angel of the nursery and the sick bed, hovering in soothing caresses over the cradle and the dying couch when all others have turned away. She ministers in tenderness of heart and sympathy of touch unto those who need her ministrations. It is the ray of sunlight when the world without is dark and

 THE SUCCESSFUL

dreary. How often has the love of woman nerved the arm of the warrior, inspired the pen of the poet, and loosed the tongue of the orator! It keeps alive the sacred fire upon the happy hearthstone, because her very heart, soul and all are bound up in her affections.

Again, note something of her affections in things divine. It might be said, and truly, that woman's affection is the vestal virgin which keeps burning the sacred fire upon the altar of her God. And without her affection for the cause of Christianity, where would we be to-day? See her as a devoted servant anointing the Saviour's feet with her tears, wiping them with the hairs of her head, and faithfully going forth in her devotion, following the Christ who redeemed her from slavery's bonds. She has ever been a loyal follower; she was the last to leave the cross, and the first to arrive at the tomb of her Lord. And what is the world without the affection of woman shining out as golden rays of sunlight into the lives of those who so much need light upon their pathway? What is the church without the tender ministrations of the heart of gentle woman? What is the cause of our Lord and Redeemer without her service? How devoted she has been in things divine, how true, loving and patient, ready always to sacrifice and to bear burdens

 YOUNG WOMAN

that she might further the cause of the Christ, and bring unto him the soul of someone she loves. How often she prays in silence and alone that loved ones might become acquainted with her Lord. Her affections! What shall we say of them? Such a theme is so deep, and so broad, and so very important that it is worthy of days and weeks of meditation by the best minds and truest hearts.

Before leaving this subject we wish to address a final word to young men: Let your conduct be always toward the young woman you meet as you would wish the conduct of other men to be toward your own sweet, innocent, and confiding sister. Then, young man, you will soon find that you are putting a premium upon the affection of true and pure womanhood, thereby making the world better, bringing heaven down to earth and carrying earth up to heaven, thus putting the love of God into human hearts in such a way that the thrill of its wondrous power is felt. May it be so with every true heart; may there be a desire strong and yearning in the bosom of every young man, and of every young woman in their relations with one another to live as God would have them live, and thereby fill a noble, honorable and upright place in the world.

VI

The Young Woman Becoming a Bride

"*For the Lord God said, It is not good that man should be alone. I will make a helpmeet for him.*"—Genesis 2:18.

"*For this cause shall a man leave his father and mother and shall cleave to his wife, and the twain shall become one flesh. What therefore God has joined together, let not man put asunder.*"—Matthew 19:5, 6.

"*To the nuptial bower
I led her, blushing like the Morn; all Heaven,
And happy constellations, on that hour
Shed their selectest influence; the Earth
Gave signs of gratulation, and each hill;
Joyous the birds; fresh gales and gentle airs
Whisper'd it to the woods, and from their wings
Flung rose, flung odors from the spicy shrub,
Disporting, till the amorous bird of night
Sung spousal, and bid haste the Evening star
On his hill-top to light the bridal lamp.*"
—*Milton.*

"*God the best maker of all marriages,
Combine your hearts in one.*"
—*Shakespeare.*

VI

THE YOUNG WOMAN BECOMING A BRIDE

MARRIAGE is a divine institution. It is not a mere human custom that has in it no sanctity or meaning, but it is heaven born, and it is one of the distinguishing features between mankind and the lower order of animals. It is the very foundation of society; without the marriage relation there could be no society; there could be no happiness of home as it is known in Christian lands everywhere. Sad it is to relate that at this day there are numbers of persons who have not considered this great question as they should, and hence do not take it with the seriousness that God intended that it should be taken. This accounts, very largely, for the unhappiness we find in so many of our homes,—for the harshness and discord in the lives of many wedded people. They have never thought seriously and prayerfully upon this holy union that is to affect their entire lives. When entering into this most sacred of all relations, the young woman should discard all thought of sensationalism, and unholy ambition, and remember that she is enter-

THE SUCCESSFUL

ing into a life partnership. Let her not forget that marriage is a contract which must not be lightly broken.

We shall consider first THE PREPARATION OF THE YOUNG WOMAN FOR BECOMING A BRIDE. This preparation is to begin under the direction of wise and discreet parents, and especially under the direction of the mother. She should be trained in domestic affairs in a way that will fit her, at the proper time, to become really and truly the manager of a home of her own. She should be able to take charge of the home and know what is expected of her and be willing to do it. Too many young women are turned out into the world who know absolutely nothing about domestic affairs. They are, as we commonly say, "upon the carpet" but know nothing about the management of a home or how to deal with those problems in the home which contributes so much towards making it comfortable and happy. With woman home ought to be the place she loves far better than any other place in the world. This is the center of her earthly being, and around it should revolve all her aspirations, and from it should come her highest joys. Just here the mother may do a great deal for the young woman,— far more, perhaps than some of our mothers

YOUNG WOMAN

realize. Listen to the wise words of a woman who had several daughters. She said: "Most parents are anxious in finding good husbands for their daughters; I am anxious in preparing my daughters to become good wives and then God will provide for them." That is really the heart of the whole matter, preparing them for this life work and then we need not fear as to the result as ordained of God.

Again, they should be taught as to the sacredness of the step; they should early have it impressed upon their hearts that marriage is the most sacred thing in all human relations. They should be taught to realize that this is ordained of Almighty God, and that it is a blending of lives henceforth, so long as they are both in the world. They should be made to realize that there must be no effort at separation so long as they both live,—save upon one Scriptural ground ,should this ever become necessary. The young woman should learn to understand what it means to give up her home, and what it means to give up her name and go out upon life's sea, and to her, an untried sea, with the one to whom she has committed herself. She should be taught to realize that this is the most solemn and sacred step which she can possibly take in all her life, since the happiness of her whole future will

THE SUCCESSFUL

depend upon the right choice at this critical moment in her career. Some of our mothers are so solicitous about getting their daughters married that they teach the young woman to become "man crazy." It is truly a very deplorable thing for a young woman to arrive at such a point or to have such a feeling. In the home training there should be proper instruction, such as will give her right ideas for founding a home of her own. She must know what a home really is if she ever hopes to manage its affairs so as to make it a comfortable and happy place. She is the proper one to manage the household but she must manage with love, skill and gentleness, so as to make the home the brightest place this side of heaven.

Then she should realize that there is need for a sympathetic and helpful nature in the home; that she is to be the companion for life of one in whom her whole hopes are bound up and with whom she is to stand in life's conflicts. Her comradeship is to contribute more sympathy and help to the husband than can come from all the world beside. In the hours of adversity when men often have become discouraged and have grown despondent because of disappointments in the great battles of life, happy are they who can come into the home

 **YOUNG WOMAN**

and there find a heart that goes out in true and tender sympathy, that they might receive courage and strength again for the battle tomorrow. A banker in a great eastern city, the head of an institution worth hundreds of thousands of dollars, had such serious reverses that failure came. On going to his palatial home he was prostrated with grief, and said to his wife "All is gone; we have lost all; they will sell everything we have." The wife said "Do you mean to say that they will take all?" He said "yes, they will take all, our beautiful home, our elegant furnishings, everything." But she said "do you mean to say that they will sell all we have?" He said "yes, all." "Husband, will they sell me, and our precious children?" "O no, wife, I don't mean that, they will take all of our property." Then she said "You have me left, you have our beautiful children left and we can start again and yet be successful in the world." That was the very thing that the husband needed, that was the thing he was thirsting for and it nerved him for a new courage and a new effort which meant future victory. How sympathetic, how helpful, and how inspiring is the companionship of a noble and true woman!

The writer once had a friend who was in trouble because of his health, and was com-

THE SUCCESSFUL

l to be away from wife and loved ones.
s absence the wife was looking after his
s, and in our correspondence he was tell-
iow faithfully his wife was discharging
uties that devolved upon her, and in one
s letters he said "A true woman is God's
gift to man." That is true beyond the
ow of doubt and would God that we might
e more than we do that this is true. The
g woman in her preparation should have
iroper vision for becoming a companion to
vith whom she has consented to go through
ourney of life. It very often happens that
g women do not realize that a man needs
ntellectual equal, one who can talk with
upon the subjects that come into the circle
is own life. He wants someone who can
e in any circle where their lot may be cast,
he will be proud of, not only on the wed-
day, but on through the days of life after
have gotten out into the thick of the
e and after they have experienced many
ie trials and troubles of life and have come
alize that life is serious and that life really
ruest.
gain, she should have the proper vision for
own self protection in choosing the right
of helper for life. One of our state legis-
res once entertained a bill to prohibit

YOUNG WOMAN

young men who are addicted to drink from becoming benedicts. This shows how some minds are thinking upon this great question.

The Czarina of Russia, while visiting at one time a school for girls, asked the young women to tell her the meaning of love, when the teacher said "They do not so much as know the word, they do not know its meaning at all, they are never allowed to know anything about that question." The Czarina replied, "They ought to know, they ought to be taught its meaning in order that they may become intelligent mothers of this country and helpful women, who are to shape in a large way the destiny of our land." Richter well asks the young women if their "hearts are of so little worth that they can cut them, like old clothes, to fit any breast." The meaning is clear that character is to count for something in the estimation of a young woman when she consents to share her lot with one for a life partner. Character is to be genuine and real, and to her it is to have meaning, and she is to let the young man understand that it must have meaning in his life.

We come now to discuss the question **WHEN SHE SHOULD BECOME A BRIDE?** First of all at the proper age. We may get into trouble just here, but ordinarily speaking, she should be out of her teens. It is often

THE SUCCESSFUL

sad to think of the little girls that are placed upon the matrimonial market, and are to take upon themselves vows for life about which they know nothing. We would not discredit the lives of those who have married under such circumstances, and have been made happy, but we would sound a note of warning among the thousands of young girls, especially in the large cities. They should take note of the many lives which have been made unhappy because they allowed themselves to be drawn into the marriage relation before they had any idea as to its requirements. The young lady ought at least to be smart enough and old enough to choose with some degree of intelligence. She should have some idea as to the vows she is taking upon herself, as to the meaning of home, the meaning of companionship, the meaning of care, and the meaning of motherhood.

Many times have we seen mothers who seemed to have one idea, and one idea only, with reference to their daughters, and that was to make for them a match. They were determined to settle this matter for them just as early as possible lest they be left in the world without a man. The matter of having a real husband seems not to be considered by such mothers. They act as if they only wanted

YOUNG WOMAN

their daughters tied to a man who might pay their board and buy their clothes. This question is too serious to be thus trifled with, and let mothers ever remember that they are not to do the loving for the daughters. She will not have to make the home for the daughter, and so the young heart ought rather to have the liberty, the right, and the privilege of choosing for herself. The mother may and should direct in the right way, but after all, she must allow the young woman to be free to settle upon some heart that she truly loves and is willing to choose for a companion in the life journey.

The young woman should be old enough to recognize character, and to really know its meaning. Then let her understand that she is not going to find character in the saloons and billiard halls, nor in the so called men's clubs of the country. She may put it down that when young men are giving themselves evening after evening to the saloons and billiard halls, that they have not the character which she should demand for a life partner. They are not proper subjects to whom she should commit herself for protector and helper and guide in life. Often it happens that young women lose sight of this. Instances of it are seen on every hand. Many cases can be

 THE SUCCESSFUL

cited where young women have been determined to marry some fellow with whom they had become fascinated. They were duly warned as to his lack of character, and of the misery that was sure to follow, and yet they would turn a deaf ear to all of these warnings. Solemn is this question, and we ought to be able to reason upon it as we would reason upon other questions. Yet it does often seem true that "love is blind and lovers cannot see."

Over and above all, the young woman when choosing a life companion should be swayed by love, not allowing herself to be married to someone merely to assume the financial obligations necessary to her existence. Her heart's desire should be to cast in her lot with some worthy man that they might be happy together, and have a real home. Home is the dearest spot in all the earth. It is a place where lives that are truly wedded delight to hide away from the world without, and there revel in the society of each other. They are supremely happy because two true hearts are bound by the golden tie of love. Here they know the meaning of genuine love, of unwavering confidence and of true esteem for each other, even though the world without may be harsh, and grating with its discords of strife. The young woman should insist on her husband provid-

YOUNG WOMAN

ing, at least during their first wedded days, a home of their own where they can live by themselves. To be sure there are times when circumstances will not permit this and proper allowance should always be made in such cases. But where it can be done, she should always desire to have a home, a place where she is mistress of the situation and where she can try her skill in creating happiness for the one she really loves.

A great many of our young people make a fatal mistake in seeking the boarding house, or some place where they will have no cares or responsibilities upon them in their early wedded life. This is especially hurtful in public boarding houses, where invariably too much jest is indulged in to leave room for the serious things of life. It is conceded that newly wedded lives have room for much poetry and fun, yet the current of seriousness must not be choked entirely. Then, too, housekeeping will give her an opportunity to use all of the nice wedding presents she has received, instead of storing them away for years in some garret, unless they be like the present a certain young woman brought to the groom, which consisted of three maiden aunts, sixteen cousins and a mother-in-law. That was rather overdoing it in one special line,—variation and scatteration

THE SUCCESSFUL

would have helped in this instance. Yet many of us have mothers-in-law that are very dear and helpful to us, and there are times untold when they prove to be ministering angels in the lives of the young people. The point to be noted, young woman, is to allow yourself to have a home where no one can enter in to take sides in any of the little difficulties that might arise. All such problems should be solved when you two are alone before God, and then you will most likely settle them right.

A young woman should not marry for position or money. The writer once knew a family in New Orleans, who lived in the most fashionable part of that great city, where palatial homes are found for miles. In a certain instance the woman wished to have her carriage for her own use, and the husband desired to have the carriage at the same hour for his use. Some contention arose over the matter and finally she said, "I have a right to it, my money bought it." Then he hurled back the cutting reply, "Yes, and your money bought me, too." There was a home palatial and elegant in all of its furnishings, yet no happiness, no joy, and no love in that home! Another instance noted is that of a young man, prominent and wealthy, who was in love with a beautiful and fashionable young

YOUNG WOMAN

woman. He was told by his friends that this girl did not love him. He protested that they did not know what they were talking about, but his friends insisted that she was marrying him only for money. Time went on, and after awhile in the business world the young man and his father had a slight reverse which amounted to but little, yet it was prominently announced in the papers. Here was his opportunity for testing her; he went to the young woman and mentioned the fact that she had doubtless seen the announcement in the paper as to his reverses, and that while they might not be able to live in the same style and luxury as formerly intended, yet he wished her to know that his love for her was the same, and that he would do his best to make her happy. The young woman said in reply to this, "But really I am sorry to hear that, you know, George, I do love you but I would make the worst sort of a wife for a poor man, and I think we had better break the engagement now." While the disappointment was keen and severe to the young man it unmistakably revealed to him that his friends were right. The engagement was broken and later he found a young woman who loved him, and married him and helped him with her love and sympathy in regaining all that was lost, while the first

 **THE SUCCESSFUL**

young woman had the chagrin of seeing her mistake. Young woman, don't let your feelings for a man rest on his fortune, or lack of fortune, but let your love be for the man himself and for your joys with a life companion.

Then in her choosing she is to choose only when true character seeks her comradeship,—avoiding the missionary spirit in getting married. Some women are foolish enough to marry men as if to reform them. Sometimes a woman says he has a good heart and he will reform for me, I know he will. No you don't! If you can't reform him before your marriage you may be sure that in nine chances to one you cannot reform him after you are married. There are some exceptions but they are not the rule, and it ought to serve to open your eyes to the situation and keep you from taking this serious step in a missionary spirit. Young woman, don't wed some disreputable, sin-besotted wretch whom you may imagine you can reform! The poor houses of our land are full of women and orphan children because of such disastrous mistakes, and the world is saying, "The mistake,—the awful mistake they made!"

Then a woman should not allow herself to be deceived by a mere flirt of the day. The young man who will allow himself to trifle with

 ## YOUNG WOMAN

a young woman's heart is himself the worst kind of a criminal and the greatest enemy to society. He is indeed and in truth the one who is guilty of bringing more unhappiness to her life than any other character that can be found. There was a young woman in one of our Southern cities, who was sought by a young man like this, and she replied by saying to him, "Yes, I can marry a man who makes love to a different girl every month, I can marry a man who stands in front of churches and makes audible remarks about people who are compelled to pass by him, I can marry a man who has no support but his aged father, I can marry a man who boasts that with the help of a good tailor and a smooth tongue that he can marry any girl he wants, yes, I can marry such a man, but I won't!" And thus she disposed of him in short order, just as a true hearted woman should dispose of every creature like that who would dare seek her hand in marriage.

Young woman, will you not realize that this is the most serious step that you can possibly take, and when once taken your life will be different ever after? In the marriage relation you are brought into touch with another life which is going to blend with yours, and if his character is degraded, so must your character

VII

The Young Woman as a Home-Maker

"She looketh well to the ways of her household, and eateth not the bread of idle —*Proverbs 31:27.*

"There's a bliss beyond all that the minstr told,
  When two, that are linked with one her tie,
With heart never changing, and brow cold,
  Love on thro' all ills, and love on til die."
                                            —,

"The reason why so few marriages are is because young ladies spend their time in ing nets, not in making cages."—*Swift.*

VII

THE YOUNG WOMAN AS A HOME-MAKER

A HAPPY home is the dearest spot in all the world. It is the brightest place this side of heaven. It brings to our minds thoughts of that better home beyond the stars of God, where all is joy and peace. There should be a sincere desire on the part of every man and woman in the land to have, and share in a place of joy and happiness, commonly called "home." God has so ordained that neither man nor woman alone can make the happiest home. In either instance when the other is absent there is something lacking. Man and woman are the complement of each other and no home is complete without both.

In the discussion of this theme we wish to think first of THE HOME AS HER BASIS OF OPERATION. God has decreed that we should have home life. God is the author and founder of the family. That being so we should endeavor to have our homes regulated according to his divine plan. This should be true with reference to motherhood; here is the place for the bearing and rearing of children. This was in God's design when founding the

THE SUCCESSFUL

home, and pitiable is the fireside that is never to hear the prattle of sweet children. Too many firesides of our land are homes only in name while in reality they are nothing more than stopping places. The very thought of children is repulsive, and the very idea of their presence, and of having their care, is so out of the question that such persons shrink from the consideration of it.

Perhaps some would say this kind of speaking is out of order upon a theme of this kind, and yet one of the worst curses of our time is the fact that we have so many childless homes. Places called home where children are absent because the wedded pair do not wish to have them. They do not desire their presence, not being willing to enter seriously into the divine plan of rearing and training children to become the future citizens of our land. Some women can love and fondle a poodle dog, when they would be horrified at the thought of becoming the mother of children. May heaven pity such unnatural creatures!

Again, the home is her basis of operation in the matter of companionship. God saw that it was not good for man to be alone and thus he created for him a companion. This companion was to be his help, his stay, his sympathy, his strength and the source of his earthly

love in its very highest form. We have some so-called homes where people are "mated" as the world chooses to say; they are tied together and held by the laws of the country. Yet in such unions there is sad lack of true companionship, and where there is lack of companionship, there must of necessity be absence of joy and love. In every real home there should be felt the thrill of companionship, one for the other, throughout life. Husband and wife should be the truest and best companions found anywhere. Each should desire the companionship of the other above the companionship of anyone else on God's earth. If this were religiously carried out in the homes of our country there would be less strife, less discord and jealousy and fewer divorces that now destroy so many homes in our nation. The lack of companionship is the chief cause of jealousy, and it becomes a most pitiable place when jealousy enthrones itself in the hearts of those who are at the head of the home. Sad days have indeed come when they cannot longer trust each other, for then the home exists merely in name, devoid of the reality.

The home is also her basis of operation in the service of the world. From here goes out into the world the best sympathy it can have. There is no sympathy like the sympathy that comes

 THE SUCCESSFUL

from one home to another. When sorrow is in the home and some messenger comes from another home bearing the breath of sympathy, it brings joy and gladness. We know then that there is truly a tie that binds hearts together stronger than the mere formality of the world. From here it is also that she dispenses charity in the very highest and truest way. No one else is so prepared to dispense real charity as the wifely heart, because she has learned that the highest happiness comes when all goes well in her own home. This experience sends her to another home as a ministering angel of charity in times of need.

Again, the home is the place where she is to serve most in the life of her husband. She must have a very large place in his life, since her influence here will have much to do with his career. Let it not be forgotten that her influence is powerful in his affairs,—more than is thought in a passing word. She is to endeavor at all times to have domestic felicity, to so live and minister in the home that there will be the truest domestic peace and joy possible. This can often be done by noting some of the practical every day things, leaving out perchance, a little of the poetry of our lives and addressing ourselves to the practical home questions. Let there be an earnest endeavor

on her part to be a neat and tasty housekeeper. By keeping things in order she will add much to the comfort and joy of the home, since few men are pleased with a slouchy housewife. She may add much also to the home's attractiveness by exercising some skill toward beautifying it. To be sure, this will have to be regulated largely by her tastes and financial resources, but there are so many ways by which an industrious and thoughtful woman can beautify her home.

Perhaps one of the most practical things that could be said as to home comforts is that she should be a good feeder. Most women have heard that "the way to a man's heart is through his stomach." There is more truth than poetry in the saying. She should learn very early that it takes more than just beaming upon William to satisfy the inner man. He will soon get tired of muddy coffee, soggy biscuits and spoiled meats, and want something more substantial, and she should early learn that to make him happy she must "feed the beast." Someone has very well said that "a nation's diet will determine very largely a nation's destiny." Physicians tell us that they can look at a person and tell pretty well what he is fed upon. Since there is some truth in this, doubtless many housewives are estimated very

 **THE SUCCESSFUL**

poorly by the medical fraternity. She ought also to learn that the average man has not an ostrich digestion; he may have for a while, but if abused it will wear out finally, and to preserve it, it is necessary for her either to be able to prepare good food herself, or at least to know when some one else can prepare it.

There is much good advice in a lecture delivered before a cooking school in one of our Eastern cities, in which the lecturer gave a recipe for cooking a husband. He said, "Some of our good women make a mistake by not learning early in the wedded relation to cook her husband. Some of them treat him like a bladder and hence try to blow him up; some of them keep him in hot water; while some will let him freeze by her general neglect and indifference; some try to stew him; and yet there are some who would endeavor to roast him; then some try to keep him by pickling. Be sure, young women, that you will not succeed along this line, but there is a way to cook him and he will be very delicious when done, as a rule, if the work is done properly. Do not go to the market for a husband, as the best are always brought to your own door; do not select him according to the silvery appearance as if you were buying mackerel, or the golden tint as if you wanted salmon; then be careful to

 YOUNG WOMAN

select for yourself because tastes differ along this line; and remember it is better to have no husband at all than not to be able to cook him.

"It is said that the best way to do the cooking is to have a preserving kettle of the finest porcelain; if this cannot be secured, earthenware will do; be sure that the linen in which you wrap him is thoroughly washed, well mended with the proper number of buttons and strings tightly sewed on; tie him in with a strong cord of comfort, since the cord commonly called duty is apt to be weak. You will have to tie him in the kettle because he, like the lobster and crab, must be cooked while alive; but it can be done if the proper care is exercised in doing it; don't forget to add a little sugar in the form of what confectioners call 'kisses,' but be sure not to use any pepper or vinegar under any circumstances; a little spice is said to be good, but must be used with special care. By no means stick any sharp instrument in him to see if he is getting tender; it is usually safe to stir him just a little, gently watching him to see that he does not become burned and crusty around the edges. He will likely sputter and sizzle some, though you need not be alarmed here because he often does this at first, but he will get over it after a while. Place him over a fire kindled with love, neat-

ness and cheerfulness, and keep him as close to it as you think is good for him, and when he is done you will find him very digestible; then he will agree nicely with you and the children and will keep as long as you want him to if you do not become careless and set him in too cold a place."

There is a great deal of good common sense in this recipe that is practical and helpful. Certainly the man who is really a man does not want to marry a woman merely to have a cook, yet at the same time he does want a wife who, if she has to do that kind of work, can do it, and if circumstances do not demand it, she can see that some one else does it well. Though the average man has learned, doubtless, to eat "what is set before him and ask no questions."

Turning now to another phase of the subject, she should be a peaceful companion in the home. "Be he king or peasant, he is the happiest man in all the world who has a peaceful home." Solomon says "A continual dropping on a very rainy day, and a contentious woman are alike." Let her always avoid the gunpowdery temperament; nor should she turn on the water works in her head too freely. Most men desire to be delivered from a fractious wife, or one who is continually crying. Unfortunately for some men, they are yoked with

 YOUNG WOMAN

women who have the dumps very often, and take to bed if they cannot carry their point. Such conduct is most unbecoming on the part of a wife, and is even childish. Those who are looking at the serious side of home life do everything possible to make each other happy, at all times and in all things. Let each word and each act be for a peaceful companionship in the home. Don't be like Mr. and Mrs. Spitfire, who were driving along the road when she said "Why can't married people trot along through life as peacefully as these horses are going?" He answered, "You forget that they have only one tongue between them."

As to religious things in the home, she is to be the husband's constant strength and help. A godless wife will lead her husband and children to the devil about as quickly as anything else in all the world. Wherever we find a home lacking in religious devotion on the part of the wife, we most always find a home where God is not honored, loved, or served by other members of the family. If she take no interest in religious worship, the family altar is not erected in her home. The influence of woman with reference to religion in the homes of our land cannot be overestimated. A nation will never become Christian as long as the mothers in its homes are infidels. There can be no Chris-

THE SUCCESSFUL

tian manhood to unfurl the banner of righteousness in any land, if children are not learning to pray at mother's knee. Heaven pity the home indeed, if the wife and mother in it be not religious.

The next main thing to be impressed upon woman is the fact that THE HOME IS THE CENTRE OF HER AFFECTIONS AND THE THRONE OF HER POWER. Here she is to exercise her creative powers in making the home a place of beauty in art, in music, in flowers, and in all that would stir the soul and make it joyful. However humble that home may be, she should strive to exercise as far as possible her creative powers in beautifying it. We have seen mere huts upon the hillside that were, to its inmates, as beautiful as a palace of paradise. And why, do you ask? Because there was in those humble homes a creative mind and an affectionate heart spent in beautifying them and making them the most attractive spot within the range of her influence and power.

Then let us suggest to the young woman that in making her home attractive, she is never to forget the attractiveness of self. The average man loves to come home once in a while and find that his wife is tidy and neat, and just a little dressed up for him; he is then reminded of how beautiful she was when courted as his

sweetheart; when he thought she was the most beautiful creature in all the world; when he thought her toilet was the most tasty that could be made this side of heaven. Some women grow thoughtless just here and act as if they thought any slouchy way would do for home and husband,—that it does not matter whether they are tidy for him at any time. Let her not understand that she is to remain on dress parade all the while and never be at ease because of him; oh no, not that, but don't let her forget that once in a while he would enjoy coming home and finding her looking like she did in the early days when he would ride ten miles through the dark any night in the week that he might enjoy her society for,—an indefinite period.

Again, love is to be exercised in the home for strength of character and purity. Upon the altar of the home is where she sheds her truest and best life blood. This is true in the life of her children; she ministers to them when they are sick, she sympathizes with, and soothes them when they are in sorrow and trouble; she will spend wakeful nights as does no other creature in all the earth, and thereby implant in the child's memory an idea of love that all time cannot destroy. It matters not how far from home the boy may go, he will look back

 **THE SUCCESSFUL**

to those days of early love when there was a ministering angel called mother, who watched about him when he was ill, who sympathized with him when the world was cold and cruel, and who early placed his feet in the paths of God.

It is the mother who opens as no other person, the windows of her being that the pure atmosphere and the bright sunlight of God's love might shine in upon her soul. A woman, chaste in word and deed, is the noblest and truest companion in life, and the very best conception that we can have, aside from our Lord himself, of the purity of God. On the other hand, when we think of opposite comparisons, the impure woman gives us the most repulsive idea of what is base, and vile, and low. The pure woman guards her home to make character strong, holding back from its portals everybody and everything that would even suggest moral decay. Without doubt the purity of the home rests mainly with the wife. The stand she takes in the home is going to determine the conceptions of purity that are instilled in the minds of those who dwell there.

Once more, the home is her throne, upon which she wields the sceptre of power for the nation's welfare. No nation can possibly become purer than its homes, and no home can

become purer than the wife of that home, so here it is that she exercises her power for the highest good of her country. Napoleon said, "What France needs is good mothers, and then we need not fear about France having good sons." Nothing truer and more vital could be said of any country.

Some years ago, when Jenny Lind was singing in the Old Castle Garden in New York, after she had rendered a number of those sublime productions by Beethoven, Handel and others and had received much applause, her mind seemed to go out to her old home. Then it was that the Swedish Nightingale seemed to plume her wings for a loftier flight, and began singing Howard Payne's "Home, Sweet Home." Almost instantly men and women shouted and wept and applauded as they had done in none of the other pieces rendered, while tears fell from the eyes of those thousands like showers of rain. It called back to them the sacred memories of home. Beethoven and Handel were thought of no more, but rather that heavenly place, that beautiful place called home, which God intended that his creatures should enjoy in this world. How beautiful is the word home! There is no other word in all language like it. It is an emblem of that eternal home beyond the stars where there are

no sorrows, no partings, no funeral processions, no graveyards, no death beds, no strifes and no turmoils, but one bright, happy, and beautiful day in the presence of God.

VIII

The Young Woman in Public Life

"Now Deborah, a prophetess, the wife of Lappidoth, she judged Israel at that time."—Judges 4:4.

"And the king loved Esther above all the women, and she obtained favor and kindness in his sight more than all the virgins; so that he set the royal crown upon her head, and made her queen."—Esther 2:17.

*"When perils men environ,
 The women show a front of iron;
 And, gentle in their manner, they
 Do bold things in a quiet way."*
—English.

"When I recover, when I possess once more a 'sound mind in a sound body,' I will earn my own living, 'pay my own way' and try to be of use in the world. It will—it shall—be better that I did not die."—Frances Willard, after a severe spell of fever.

VIII

THE YOUNG WOMAN IN PUBLIC LIFE

IN the presentation of this theme there is no desire to discuss the boisterous woman suffragist, but rather the modest woman who wields her influence in a more effective way as wife, mother, reformer, and queen. We do not wish to be put on record as being opposed to woman suffrage, but we are certainly out of sympathy with many of the methods used by some to achieve that end. It is true that woman in almost every age has had some part in public affairs; it is quite true also that there have been certain periods of history when she has had much more to do in these matters than at other periods. But there has perhaps been no time in all history when she has had more influence in public affairs than she has today. When given an opportunity she exercises her powers with telling effect upon most all public questions.

Let us note first, HER CAPABILITIES FOR PUBLIC GOOD. This is seen in the fact that the very nature of woman makes it possible. Her kindness and purity of heart are such that she cannot do other than exercise a very im-

 THE SUCCESSFUL

portant influence in public affairs. Whereve[r] you find the heart of a true woman you find [a] heart that is more responsive to the needy an[d] distressed, and to the oppressed than you fin[d] anywhere else; the heart of woman is tendere[r] than the heart of man, not only in the affairs o[f] home, but also in public affairs. In fac[t] wherever her influence is felt at all, this is see[n] to be true. God so created her that such shoul[d] be the case. Then her powers of intuition ar[e] such that she must of necessity have an in[1]portant influence in public life. Where me[n] very often worry over questions that arise, sh[e] will decide the matter forthwith, and if he[r] advice is followed, as a general thing, one wi[ll] be directed aright.

It is often the case that she has weighty in[1]fluence among business men. The writer ha[s] a special friend, who in a number of importan[t] instances was besought by his wife not t[o] engage in certain questionable transaction[s.] Instead of following her advice he had his wa[y] and failed, and in every single instance h[e] would have succeeded had he taken her advic[e] and each of these transactions involved larg[e] amounts of money. Examples like this serv[e] to show us that woman's intuition is suc[h] that she can often lay hold of a proposition an[d] see through it, while many men delay an[d]

worry and fret over it. In the companionship of men her influence must of necessity mingle with his thinking and acting upon public questions. It would be a very poor kind of companion whose influence was not, in some way at least bound up in the life of the other companion, and of necessity the thinking of one will influence the thinking and planning of the other.

It is observed again that her position in molding the character of each generation is such that her influence for public good is large indeed. Looking back into the early centuries, it is learned that Chrysostom, the great preacher, was made what he became largely by the influence of his mother, a woman who was especially gifted; a woman of culture and means, her husband having died early after marriage, leaving her with this child. She turned away from other offers of marriage to devote her whole life to the service of God and the training of her son, and he grew to be the greatest preacher of his time. Every historian today takes note of the work of Chrysostom, and going behind that, he sees there the expression of his mother's heart and life permeating his thought and work as he became famous in the world's history. Most Americans know how indelibly President McKinley had his

 **THE SUCCESSFUL**

mother's influence impressed upon him; after he became President of the United States, he went home to his mother and knelt down and placed his head in her lap, asking that she lay her hand on his head and pray for him as she did in his childhood days. Witnessing such a scene as this we need not wonder that he became one of the greatest men this nation has ever produced, for woven into the very fiber of his being there was the womanly influence of a precious Christian mother, and it shone out through all his deeds as a public man. This explains why both North and South mourned so sincerely when William McKinley was assassinated.

Let us consider also HER OPPORTUNITIES FOR PUBLIC GOOD. These are manifest because of the enlargement of her sphere from the home outward; she is now liberated from the false idea that her domain is bounded by four walls and a door, and a few narrow windows that are to serve as mere peep-holes through which she might look out into the world. We do not mean to get away from the idea that the first and most important place of woman is in the home, since this is the divine plan and must not be lost from view. At the same time she can work from the home outward, and can exercise an influence for public

 YOUNG WOMAN

good such as she could not possibly do in the past, for the reason that she was regarded as little more than the merest kind of servant or even a slave. But happily that day has gone and now she has larger opportunities than ever before.

Then from the school upward she may fit herself for a place of honor and renown in the great world about her. The time is not far distant in the past when men would say "Let's educate our boys for important places." But it is a comparatively recent thing for them to be heard saying "Let's educate our girls too and give them a chance, by fitting them to occupy an honorable station and fill a place that will remunerate them when they are left in the world to shift for themselves." We cannot refrain from saying to parents who read these lines that you should throw about your daughter the safeguard of an education that she may have an opportunity to honorably and nobly make her own way, if need be, and in no wise jeopardize her character. The day has truly come when there are colleges for women in our country that are affording them the best opportunities to fit themselves for important places in life. In intellect she is no longer considered the plaything of a treacherous monarch in the home, but she is reckoned

 THE SUCCESSFUL

as his equal, not only socially, but intellectually, and she is capable of exercising an influence for public good as great, and often greater than can men.

Again, her opportunities are enlarged because of the recognition of her executive ability. There have been some great women rulers in the world and not all of them have been upon a nation's throne. Many of them have been rulers in private homes, and many of them have been rulers in communities. though those we most generally hear about have been rulers in a world-wide way. When we think of the executive ability of womankind many of us turn to Queen Victoria as our ideal. She was the greatest queen that ever wielded the scepter of a throne. Each time one studies her life he finds it refreshing and interesting, and is convinced more and more that she was the mightiest power for good that ever exercised an influence in the British Empire. When the auspicious moment arrived for her to become Queen of England, the Archbishop of Canterbury and some others with him went at five o'clock in the morning to announce to Victoria that she was Queen. They were told by a servant that she was enjoying a sweet sleep and could not be disturbed, but the Archbishop said "I have come

 YOUNG WOMAN

to see the Queen of England, and her sleep must give way to this." She was then immediately called, nor did she keep them waiting long, and her first words, after having been notified that she was Queen, were to the Archbishop, when she said "I beg your Grace to pray for me," and he did and that most fervently. Thus it was that she began her most eventful reign, and her rule of more than fifty years was the brightest and most prosperous that England ever saw. Myriads of her deeds of kindness stand out before the world portraying the character, and revealing the great heart of this great woman. At one time a requisition was presented to her to sign for the execution of a soldier who had thrice deserted the army; when she asked if there was nothing about the man to recommend him, she was told that he had deserted the army three times. But upon her further insistence it was finally said "We have heard that he was a good citizen and a good man in his home but we know that he is a very poor soldier." The Queen said "Thank you," and immediately wrote across the paper "Pardoned," and signed "Victoria" after it. This act showed that she was searching for something responsive in the accused life that she might give him another chance.

 **THE SUCCESSFUL**

This noble Queen was a constant Bible reader, and often said that England had become great and happy by a knowledge of the true God through Jesus Christ. There has perhaps, never served in public life a more devout and consecrated woman than Queen Victoria, nor one who exercised an influence more far reaching for good than hers, which will live long, long after the deeds of most rulers have been forgotten. An interesting case was recently presented to our President, wherein a man who had been sentenced to death had asked for pardon. After the papers were looked over by the Chief Executive, the decision was reached not to interfere; he then asked his wife to look over the papers, and after she had gone over them carefully the sentence was commuted to life imprisonment. This is but another evidence that women still have important influence in public affairs, and far more than some of us realize.

Again we notice her influence in reform movements. There has lived one woman in this country who was designated the "Uncrowned Queen." That woman was Frances Willard, in many respects the greatest woman that America has ever produced. She went from one end of this broad land to the other, pleading for reform, and the general betterment of man-

YOUNG WOMAN

kind, by turning men away from the curse of the drink habit. Her statue is the only one today of a woman that adorns the Hall of Fame in our National Capitol.

For alleviating the suffering of mankind we note Florence Nightingale making herself famous first in the Crimean War, and who afterward became one of the greatest characters to be found. Her recent death has put the whole world in mourning. It is said that when Florence Nightingale went into the battlefields and into the hospitals among the wounded soldiers during the Crimean War, that the heart of all England went with her. A soldier in writing back home, speaking of her said, "She would speak to one and smile and nod to many others, but she could not do it all, for we lay there in great rows, but we would kiss her shadow as it fell upon us, and then lay our heads upon our pillows again content." In following up the life work of this great woman in matters which concerned the suffering public at large, one is amazed at the far reaching reforms and the great tasks she accomplished by creating a public conscience for alleviating suffering humanity.

Then we feel woman's power in the service of God. We can readily see how this is true by looking at some of the women mentioned in

 **THE SUCCESSFUL**

the Scriptures, such characters as Sarah, Rachel, Rebekah, Naomi, Ruth, Elizabeth, Mary, Lydia, Phoebe, and numbers and numbers of others, who exercised a most wholesome influence in the service of Almighty God. In her consecration, what an important part she has had in the reformation of mankind! We note here the name of Katherine Booth, who was one of the pioneer women in reaching out among the poor and giving to them the gospel, together with her help and encouragement for their general well-being. Lucretia Mott was another great reformer whose life work began seriously after the death of her only son.

Finally, in looking at SOME NOTABLE EXAMPLES, we behold a great array of women who, in other days, have been prominent in public affairs. Both Deborah and Queen Esther stand out in Bible history as women whose influence, thrown about their own people at a critical time, saved them from destruction. In later times there were the two Catherines of Russia, not exemplary moral characters it is true, but women exceptionally great in executive ability. There was also Madame de Maintenon of France, wife of Louis XIV, who as his companion through a number of years was his most trustworthy adviser in the affairs of state, and the one to whom he always turned

YOUNG WOMAN

in every difficult problem which confronted him. And had it not been for the influence of Isabella of Spain, the ships of Columbus might never have started across the seas. Then there was Elizabeth of England, holding the reins of government and ruling her people with a mighty arm; a great intellect, and in some respects a woman of great heart; but she must of necessity give first place to Victoria, whose leadership and rule have been the most powerful, wholesome and loving of any Queen who ever sat upon England's throne.

In literature, woman has played an important part. Madame de Stael, Mary A. Livermore, Elizabeth Barrett Browning, Louisa M. Alcott, "George Elliot," and Jean Ingelow are among those who have been especially prominent. In art we see Harriett G. Hosmer, Elizabeth Butler, and Rosa Bonheur; in philanthropy, Elizabeth Fry, and our own beloved Miss Helen Gould, who is today regarded the first woman in the whole world in philanthropy, and the one justly entitled to occupy the first place in that sphere. She is doubtless doing more good with her vast wealth than scores of other wealthy families in America combined. All honor to this noble woman.

In the various walks of life large armies of splendid women can be found. Frances

CPSIA information can be obtained
at www.ICGtesting.com
Printed in the USA
BVOW06s1255071117
499662BV00029BA/1560/P